Elements of Buying

Elements of Buying

(A "How To" Advertising Reference

Guide for Business Owners)

By: Adele M. Lassere

To my husband, Al, who believe it could be done!

My fond appreciation to:

- *Stan Ferrell for your continuous support, friendship over the years and the design of my cover*

- *Jason Uzarraga for your willingness to participate in my project and layout my cover*

- *Jose Villanueva came late to the project and was instrumental in assisting with the interior layout*

- *Vadrina James Johnson, small business owner, who reviewed my book and provided valuable insights on small business owners needs*

CONTENTS

Page

Introduction

Over the years, friends and acquaintances have asked me on how to purchase advertising for their business, I usually have to ask a few questions before I could give them an answer. Recently, I have received a lot more people asking me the same questions. Now, I am prompted to write this book in an effort to reach out to as many business owners who are struggling with the same questions. Many of you may not know someone in the Advertising Industry to get that expert opinion or gain general guidance on who you should hire to assist you. This book will not make you an instant pro. However, you will at the very least know how to start the process and have confidence that you can finish it.

Think of this book as a handy digest, a reference guide to help you each step of the way. Look for highlighted sections of information that will be captioned as:

- Call-outs
- Illustrations
- Research
- Tips

It is my hope that you will come to find it very useful and a benefit to your company.

Chapter 1

What's the Problem?

Congratulations, you have a business and now it time for you to advertise your "gold mine". However, you aren't quite sure how to advertise it; especially with a small budget. No worries! You have come to the right place. You can achieve your goals with some savvy footwork.

First, ask yourself, "What's the problem?" What are you trying to solve. Do you need store traffic? Is it creating awareness because you are new? Are sales just plain slow? Whether you are retail outlet with a tangible product or even if you offer a service that is intangible that can only be experienced, regardless of the scenario your business fits in, there are always solutions.

When operating your business for any time period generating traffic is crucial. You may be asking yourself: "how?" Well, the "how" to generate traffic will involve one or all of the following scenarios.

- o Awareness
- o Product differentiation
- o Location

We will explore each one of the above scenarios. Let's address *awareness* first. Awareness has to be created somehow. For instance, one school of thought is to generate "word of mouth." It can be a driver, at times, depending upon the product and what excitement surrounds your product. However, word of mouth does not always travel as quickly as one would like it. Basically, word of mouth must translate into sales at some point. Therefore, advertising becomes a very effective means to spread the word quickly to a large audience, generate interest and encourage many potential customers to visit or call on your establishment. .

Product differentiation can also impact your business. If you are selling popcorn bowls and so are ten other businesses,

"What makes your popcorn bowls the best?" How is your offering different from the other ten stores selling popcorn bowls? You have to define your product and illustrate how it is better or different from any other. It is best to research your competitor's popcorn bowls. This is what you need to investigate:

1. See how your competitors popcorn bowls are made
2. What price is it being sold at
3. Observe your competition's customer base (age group, how much they are buying, etc.)

All of these variables add up and assist you in positioning your product or service in a unique and creative manner that appeals to customers you are seeking.

Location, location, location is everything!! Just as it holds true for buying a house in the right neighborhood within the right school district and close to shopping and a major interstate artery, the same holds true for your business. If you are located out of the way, you have to generate a reason for someone to travel out of the way to come to your business. Out of the way locations, typically, means you have to become a "destination" for your customer. When you are a "destination" there are usually other descriptors that define your business. These descriptors can be anything from: upscale, unique, one-of-a-kind, the "it" place or some other descriptive that makes it worth the while to take a trip to get to you.

Illustration:

I once, interviewed with a company whose owner was a construction magnet in Atlanta. He is the largest African-American owned Construction Company in Atlanta, if not also in the United States. He had invested in this restaurant that he dubbed as an upscale sports bar, which offered banquet area for weddings and/or private parties. This sports bar had all of the above problems: lack of awareness, product differentiation and location was a major issue too. It was located near Atlanta's convention center area. It is in an area that is slowly being revitalized. And, if the business could survive long enough to wait through the revitalization, the area would eventually prove to be a good location. However, they still had the awareness and product differentiation. In my interview, I

4

suggested that they would need to make it a destination. A place worth the drive out of the way especially if nothing was going at the convention center or sporting facilities. I also advised that they should purchase radio, especially jazz formatted stations, and negotiate remotes with the buy in order to generate traffic to the location. Since, they had low awareness, not enough of their potential customers knew they were there. Buying radio would assist in alleviating the awareness problem. The product was really no different from going to any other sports bar or restaurant in the Atlanta area. Another suggestion I offered was for them to contact major corporations in the Atlanta area and advise them about their banquet facilities. A smart collateral piece could be developed to send out to these companies; per my recommendation. By soliciting these companies to host their meeting and/or holiday event at the restaurant/bar's banquet room, would yield bookings for the banquet room that was virtually unused. Just in case you are curious on whether I got the job or not, my salary was a bit high for them. However, I did hear of their advertising on radio (jazz station) later where they were using remotes to buildup the excitement and make the restaurant/bar a "destination."

As you can see by this illustration, all three of these scenarios are inter-related after all. They have to coexist with each other in order to bring about the results you are looking for. At the end of the day, you must find a "real" or at the very least a "perceived" difference of what makes your product or service better and then creates the awareness of it. When you are experiencing slow sales and you have done everything imaginable from reducing price, to coupons, other gimmicks and still nothing works, it still goes back to one or all three scenarios: lack of awareness, lack of product differentiation or location. If it walks like a duck and quacks like a duck, it is still a duck. You still are selling a duck that is not "perceived" to be different. Perception from the consumer (or customer) is everything. Whether it's a right perception or not, the old adage applies, the customer is always right. So, right now you are asking, how do we address these concerns? Well, that's why we have a chapter two: "who's your customer."

Chapter 2

Who's Your Customer?

The mistake most businesses make is that they believe "everybody" is their customer. Even if you are selling detergent to clean clothes, everybody doesn't automatically become your target. Detergent uses are markedly different. Case in point: One user may want a detergent that is formulated for sensitive skin with no fragrances or other additives. Another user may want a detergent that is not harmful to the environment. A mother shopping for a family of four may just want a cheap price. See how a simple thing such as detergent became complicated by preference of the customer?? This commodity product has just diminished the total number of customers all based on preferences of the customer. Hence, everybody is not your target. In this world of many choices that we have evolved into, your customer base is not always defined as a mass group. Instead it may be a much smaller group then you think.

Tip

You cannot be all things to everybody. However, you can consistently have your company be apart of or at the top of the consideration list to a targeted group of buyers.

Now, make no mistake, I am not implying that you cannot use mass media to target a niche audience. You can, you just have to be wise about how you spend your hard earned revenue. There will be more on this later.

How do you determine who is your customer. Whether you have been in business awhile or just starting out, you have a wealth of knowledge already working on your behalf. Whether you have an existing customer base or not, ask customers coming into your establishment a few basic questions at checkout:

- o How did you hear about us?
- o What keeps you coming back to us?
- o How can we improve your experience with us?

o   May we have your email address?

It will assist you in gaining insights to your customer. Look at the age group coming into your business. In many cases you can tell if your product or service is skewing older or younger. If you believe you have an older customer base and now you're seeing younger customers, you need to ask that younger customer, what's bringing them in? Somewhere along the line, there was either a shift in how you are doing business or the product is now somehow more youthful. This shift could have been so subtle that even you didn't realize it happened.

A decision needs to be made about whom you want to cater to. Before you make that decision you need to understand some basic dynamics about older and younger customers. Based on my 20+ years of experience, below provides research facts covering a few core groups that are typically targeted for a variety of products and/or services. Best part about it, you benefit from my experience and don't have to pay a research company for it.

Research

Let's explore the three (3) core groups. These groups have been put together because the individuals within the group have similar age, lifestyle and psychographic patterns. Groups are defined as:

- **Baby Boomers**
  - Born between 1946 – 1964
  - This group has had the most attention from manufacturers and service-oriented companies because they are viewed as the largest demographic group actively buying in the marketplace. However, the younger boomer generally does not view themselves as having much in common with their older boomer. If you were born 1961-1964, younger boomer would sometimes describe them as Generation X (Gen X) or even believe they are both Baby Boomer and Gen X.

- **Generation X**
  - Born between 1965 – 1979
  - Gen Xers tend to have a large amount of discretionary dollar at their disposal. This is true

primarily due to the life cycle they have reached where heavy spending occurs. This generation has actually entered into the homebuyer market at a much earlier age than the previous generation. Therefore industries associated the home building have benefitted; such as home improvement. Items that are geared towards children are of importance to this group since many have children.

- **Generation Y (The Millennials)**
  - o Born between 1980–1995
  - o Now this generation really doesn't have much in common with Gen Xers. This group tends to be very high-maintenance, high belief in their own self-worth and demand high performance. Many Gen Y parent's overindulged their children every whim. You will find in this generation that they will challenge the status quo in the workplace and tend to purchase items based on their peers' influence. This groups is also very tolerant of workplace diversity

As you can see these group of consumers are very different in their behavioral patterns. Depending on your product or service you need to factor in their ideals of how they view themselves which directly correlates to how and what they buy.

On the horizon, is an emerging consumer group that comprises 12-34 year olds; 19.6 million based on US census data. (Note: This demographic crosses two generations; Gen Y and Millennial.) They will also be ethnically diverse who will not only admire but rather earn their money as a business or entertainment moguls instead of a traditional occupation, such as medical or legal professionals. This group will be hip-hop focused and will not fit within the normal urban demographic. Many are likely to live in the suburbs and are white. They will place a high emphasis on their on self-worth and influence. (Many of you may have worked with one in the past.)

This is a group that tends to be on the cutting edge of technology and will be early adopters of technological products, clothing trends, etc. The best thing this group has going for themselves is their ability to instantaneously make a product or service a hit. They use technology to generate what we in advertising call "viral marketing." This is word of month advertising but it spreads faster than the speed of light over the Internet, cell phones, text messages, social websites (like Facebook) etc. There is a tendency for this group to overspend for items just for the sake of being "first". But, no sooner the fad (or trend if you will) is over and gone, these early adopters, of course, are on to the next new thing. Fickle is a good word for this younger demographic group. In order to continue advertising (or marketing) to them, you must stay ahead of the trend curve. This could be pretty exhaustive work unless you love a challenge and consider yourself a trendsetter. However, if you are settled in your ways, I don't think you would have the energy level needed to keep up with this group.

This group, generally speaking, tends to consume the following media vehicles:

o High users of the Internet

o Low users of newspapers; unless online

o Females will be avid readers of magazines compared to Males

o High users of Outdoor which includes nontraditional outdoor such as: bathroom advertising in restaurants/bars or GameStop™, gaming retailer in the country

o Moderate television users

- o Heavy radio listeners (especially, online and satellite)

Baby Boomers tend to be very discriminating with their spending. They are in a different life cycle so depending if children are present in the home, they may sacrifice quality for quantity. If no children are present, they may opt for quality over quantity. But, in either case "value" comes into play. Now "value" can mean a lot of things. Value can be, I'll spend more for consistent service or purchase of a product. The perception of service must be consistent and they will continue to return because of that "value". Value can be, I need to get the most for my dollar and/or save some money. So, service level and/or quality of product may not be important because here quantity is more important than saving money. Value can also mean, I do not mind spending a lot for a luxury product or service provided I perceive it to be worth the value of the money I am spending. See how "value" means different things to different people within this same group.

This group, generally speaking, tends to consume the following media vehicles:

- o Moderate to Heavy users of the Internet
- o Moderate to Heavy users of newspapers
- o Females will be avid readers of magazines compared to Males; although, Males will read more business-related and sports publications
- o High users of Outdoor which includes nontraditional outdoor such as: advertising in movie theaters
- o Moderate to heavy television viewers (If there are children present and you have a stay at home mom, tend to be heavy daytime television viewers and moderate to light primetime television viewers depending on how old the children are.)
- o Moderate to Heavy radio listeners (If they are professional adults, they will spend a lot of time commuting in their cars and/or via public transit. Tendency to listen to music. Many public transit commuters have converted their listening to their mp3 players.)

15

Illustration

Let's look at an example that is near and dear to my heart: "shopping." You have many large department stores in the United States. Each of them, attempt to differentiate themselves from the next one. With the following example, I will provide generic names to actual department stores. My rationale for this is I do not want to be perceived as endorsing one over the other. One department store, let's call it "Department Store A" may have excellent service and a fantastic shoe selection. It prices tend to be moderate to high. Another department store, let's call it "Department Store B" may be known for having higher quality products and one of a kind products. However, their prices tend to be high. Let's lump all other department stores together. Let's call them "Department Store C and D" as offering some exclusive lines carried but pricing and quality is standard. Both of these stores offer low to moderate pricing. Occasionally a certain item may be offered at a higher price. Would anyone really know the difference if you purchased a blouse from Department store C or D? Looking at it, one would have surmised that you could have purchased it from either one. However, Department Stores C and D both actively market their perceived difference from each other. The question becomes can your customer tell the difference?? This is the reason it is important to target your audience (customer) and develop a compelling attribute that will keep that customer shopping with you. You do not want to be considered homogeneous (the same). From my personal shopping experience, Department Store A has built a reputation on shoes. When they expanded their offerings, service became a key point of difference. They have a staff that is very customer sensitive. I can buy shoes cheaper and maybe even the exact same style and brand at a shoe warehouse. However, I wouldn't get the service that Department Store A offers.

Department Store B on the other hand, tends to cater to a whole another echelon. Its prices are notably higher than Department Store A in many instances. Yet, their perceived difference is providing one-of-a-kind or very exclusive items. An experience comes to mind, when I was still in college in Houston, Texas. A

friend dragged me into Department Store B to buy this purse.
As a person along for the ride, I was picking up and examining
several items. I must admit my mouth dropped open on the
price tags attached to these exclusive items. Again, I was on a
college budget at the time. My friend on the other hand,
obviously did not perceive herself to be on a college budget;
even though she and I earn about the same amount of money.
But, I was knocked off my feet when my friend purchased this
$500 hand-painted cigar box purse. How many of you
remember that fad back in the early 80's?? She put it on her
credit card. If it were up to me, I would have had the men in the
white jackets come and take her away before spending $500 on
this purse when she still had books to buy for her classes.
While many of our friends were buying the knock-off, she
wanted the original. Like a person drinking a full-bodied
cabernet of brand A that has a 95 rating, you wouldn't be able to
tell the difference where it is purchased unless you were there.
However, in this instance, you could taste the difference. I
guess, in the end, the only thing that mattered was she was
pleased with her purchased, which set her apart from the

masses. She had a designer exclusive. I am sure that purse has long been buried and like all must have purchases yielded to the next thing in must-have.

There you have it in black & white. At the end of the day, department stores are selling a perceived difference. As an owner, you must evaluate who your customer is and actively market a perceived difference between you and your competitor. And you must select media vehicles (TV, radio, newspaper, outdoor, online, etc.) that your customer's actively use.

This is a good spot to move into the next chapter. You have learned some basics about your customers, the generation that customer falls within and insights on the importance of how to extend an invitation to customers to buy your product and/or service differentiating your product and/or service. Next an evaluation is needed on

Chapter 3

How To Reach Your Customer

Remember, you started asking your current customers what they like about your product/service. You've collected several responses. Hopefully, you have compiled these responses and kept track. These responses are what we call primary research. The responses are data, in essence. NOTE: If you just started your business, the principles are basically the same. I will provide more information on this in a bit.

These responses should give you inkling as to what appeals and to whom it appeals to. Always ask:

1) How did you hear of us?

2) Returning customer, "What keeps you coming back?"
   This is a question that can be asked in conversation.

3) How can we improve our offering for you?

There are many more questions that can be asked. But, you get the point that I am attempting to make. All of these provide clues. In the ad (advertising) game, we always deemed primary research as the best. It's straight from the horse's mouth.

Illustration

Before moving on, let's pause to set up a scenario for a new business owner. Your business has no awareness. You're new with no customers to speak of. Where do you start? You start with:

1) What product/service am I selling?

2) Who would this appeal to?

3) Do I offer any unique benefit? Or do I need to create a "perceived" difference?

Now, if you really pause to contemplate the above, it's clear before you opened for business there was a need to offer this product/service. In your marketing plan, you believed that this product/service was needed by some set of consumers. So, this preliminary becomes the starting point of defining your audience; a.k.a. customer.

Let's use a computer store opening to illustrate the point further. You opened a computer repair store. Given how fast technology is changing and the need for technicians, who can repair computers operational problems, does sounds like a smart idea. Right off the batting plate, you are competing with Big Box stores who offer Geek Squad™ services and other mom & pop outfits offering a similar service. How can you compete?

Elementary my dear Watson, you immediately look for points of difference. It could be any or all of the following:

1) Service can be stressed.

2) Convenience in terms of location.

3) Fast return, pick-up service, in-home service are a few more.

Let's say your target is Adults with computers. Well, that's pretty broad. From a spending standpoint you may not be able to spend the amount needed in advertising to reach all adults who own a computer. So, let's see if we can break this down into a manageable chunk. Let's say you want adults who own a computer within 20 miles of your location. Well, that narrows it down a bit and it becomes more manageable on what you can possible afford to spend to reach the target. Let's also say you want them to have disposable income where they will seek service often for upgrades in addition to repairs. Any time you start adding the word "disposable income" you are seeking someone with discretionary funds. But, this is also someone who also places value on his or her money. In Chapter 2, we saw clear differences between age groups; Baby Boomers, Generation X and Y.   Within Gen X and Y, are subgroups of 12-34 year olds who cross both groups."

For the purposes of this exercise, we will say that Adults 25+ who own a computer and live within 20 miles of your location are your target. Now you might say, why not 18 years olds. They are tech savvy and love gadgets galore. This is all true. However, the question becomes: "How many 18 year olds will repair the computer vs. going out and buying the latest and hottest computer? After all, the research provided in Chapter 2, pointed to this defined differences, as well as, these 18 years have less of life's responsibilities on their shoulders, typically. They also tend to be a bit freewheeling with their spending; whereas, an older adult will think of the repair option first before buying a new computer. Unless of course, the computer is several years old and it is time to get a new one.

Do you see the point I am making? The idea is to figure out who would offer more opportunity for repeat business. After all, your stomach does prefer to have food in it everyday. So, you need customers coming in every day to keep your belly full. This keeps the "OPEN" sign on your door.

Now you have your target or customer. You just need to see what your point of difference is. If you have an out of the way location, you may need to make your business worth the trip or have some clear point of difference. This is when you go check out your competitors and evaluate their services. There is nothing wrong with scoping out the competition. A little recon can go a long way. In the world of advertising, we do it all the time. I can't tell you how many times I played a college student or interested buyer in my past lives. Then you can use this information to determine what you can do to create, if necessary, your perceived difference. All of this works in unison to determine what will be the selling point to grab your customer's attention and make them buy and continue to buy.

Collecting your customer's email address would allow you to send out an e-newsletter (email newsletter) or sale promotion to your customers with some frequency. It would help you to build loyalty. Additionally, you can consider starting a loyalty program where after so many visits the customer receives 10% off or offering some sort of drawing and/or supporting some community activity by offering say $1 going to the local high school band for uniforms. This is just food for thought to help you start thinking about what distinguishes you from the rest of the pack.

Now that we have collected data from the customer by asking questions, how do you reach the audience (customer)? First you must start with how much can you spend on advertising. There are many rules of thumb ranging from % of Sales to % of Net Revenue or just plain I will only spend "X" amount this year. Once you determine what amount is best for you, you will need to consider the following:

- If you haven't scheduled any advertising and the customer who stopped in just happen to see your store because you were in a strip mall with a larger retailer (typically the anchor store), then the location you selected is in a pretty high traffic area and you are riding off of the anchor store's traffic. In many cases, you believe you are breaking even and may believe that you still need more revenue in order to show a profit. Then advertising is viable option to increase that traffic. If you are showing a profit and want more, then advertising is a viable option for you. As my mother always advised me growing up, "you get what you pay for!" Here are a few situations you may have experienced in the past:

- If you have scheduled advertising in the past but didn't believe it worked as well as it could have, you now have this guide to share more insights. You will need to evaluate where you spent your money. Was it in TV, Cable, Radio, Newspaper, etc.? How much did you spend? The rule of thumb is you need to have some degree of frequency in order to break through the clutter. For instance, if you only spent $4,500 on a one-week schedule in TV, then of course, it won't yield the results you were looking for. There wasn't enough frequency to break through the clutter that is on TV. Conversely, if it was spent on Radio for a promotion with a remote (DJ from the station is at your location for 2-3 hours advising your potential customers what is going on special that day at your location), then you could have experience traffic coming in during that weekend and possibly the following week or two after the remote. See what a difference on what type of media selected can make.

- If you spent it on one newspaper ad in the major daily in your market (city), then you need to ask:

- o How many times did you run the ad?

- o What size was it?

- o Where did you place it? Running a small ad in the newspaper, once, would in many cases not yield you any tangible results.

TIP

You must also keep in mind who you are targeting and what media they prefer.

People are creatures of habits. And, your customers will have their favorite media, or if you prefer, where they like to get information. This is a key point that in any planning you do to advertise your business that you include a website. With gas prices at an all-time high, gone are the days of driving everywhere first. Most of your customers will start, and in some cases, stop with the Internet. So, a good website would help illustrate your brand and your product and/or service offerings. (Yes, your store is a brand you are selling.)

Chapter 4

Mining the Maze of Advertising Choices

We are at the stage where we need to make a deal with a media partner.

TIP

FORGET ABOUT WHAT YOU LIKE! IT IS NOT ABOUT YOU.

It's about your target audience (customer).

Many owners get trapped in the mode of the media choices they sometimes tend to embrace their likes vs. their customers likes. Therefore, you must remember you are trying to gain customers and doing what you notice doesn't always translate into sales from your customers.

Illustration

Case in point, many years ago, I worked on what was then the #4 beer brewer in the country. We had, as part of, the advertising spending: "coop dollars". These are dollars that the beer distributors kick in to contribute to local advertising. Of course, the Agency, along with other Agencies including me would put these local plans together and present to the distributors for approval. In most cases, their monies were mainly going to be used for radio, outdoor and in some cases, sport packages for professional sport teams. This one distributor in North Carolina wanted me to use a specified outdoor company. This outdoor company had a location right outside of his distributor location. Now, the product advertised on the outdoor billboard was targeting African-Americans. As you might surmise, the beer distributor was located in an industrial park that was miles away from the trading area that the target would be frequenting. Of course, I advise against this move. Remember, the old adage: "The customer is always right." I placed the board right outside his distributorship, as he demanded. Yes, he was impressed by the fact that every morning coming into his location, he saw the billboard. Hey, I was tickled pink if he was. Of course, I knew this would be short lived. About 6 weeks later, I get a call from the owner of this distributor complaining that his volume being pulled in by the local retail outlets was down. You can guess what happened next. Yes, he wanted the billboard moved to the retail trading area. Of course, as the dutiful Agency planner moved it without even a whimper of the "I told you so!" At least not to the Client that is!!

Moral of the Story: DO NOT FALL into the trap of you having to see your ad and not your customer's seeing it!!

Let's move on. Let's discuss the many choices of advertising. I feel compelled to provide an overview of the various types of media. Mainly, the world of advertising is evolving at lightning speed. There are many choices available and fall within a few groups: Traditional, Non-Traditional and Emerging Media (Online). You will find that the currency of exchange (the way you buy it) becomes markedly different between the various groups. Within the Traditional media, you will find that the way it is purchased is basically the same from each type of vehicle. Conversely, Non-Traditional and Emerging Media will vary from type to type. Let's review the types that fall within each group and the media math (the formulas will be included in order for you to see how the cost is figured out:

a) Traditional vehicle includes: television (including cable), radio, outdoor (billboards), newspapers, and magazines. These vehicles are mass media, which means they reach everyone. The only targeting of specific audiences that these types of media can accomplish comes down to television program selected (or cable network selected) or with radio stations format to sections of the newspaper purchased to type of magazines. **NOTE: Television is broken into two (2) categories; over-the-air stations, such as: CW, NBC, FOX, etc., to cable networks, such as: TNT, SPIKE, SCFI, etc.** Each of these vehicles will attract a certain audience (or customer) that you are seeking. It is just a matter of determining, which will suit your purposes best. Buying a market such as Atlanta, you can purchase television, cable and radio based on a cost-per-spot basis. For instance, it may cost you $1,500 to purchase one spot on American Idol in your market because your targets (customer) of Adults

18-49 like to watch that show. Of course, you can purchase a show that is cheaper, but it may take more spots just to garner the audience totals (viewership) that this show draws. Outdoor (billboards) and print are priced by the unit. If you want a 25% showing of outdoor in your market, it may take 5 boards to reach the 25% showing of the audience (customer) your are targeting. Therefore, it may cost you $2,000 per billboard and you need 5 billboards for a 25% showing that will cost you a total of $10,000 to purchase 5 units or boards per month. **NOTE: Formula: Cost per billboard x the number of billboards = total cost. Be aware that production for outdoor will be in addition to the space cost. Based on this fact, it is best to only use outdoor if you plan to be up longer than a month. Given the production cost, you want to gain some efficiency by being up longer than a month. In other words, you want to ensure your ROI is realized by advertising longer than a month. It is recommended to have the creative up for at least three (3) months.** As for print,

Magazines and Newspapers are purchased by units too. So, a Half Page ad may cost you $1,500 per insertion (or each time you run the ad. **NOTE: Newspapers, generally, speak in Per Column Inch (PCI) rates. So, a Half Page unit in newspaper will most likely end of being 6 columns x 10.5". So, if the newspaper is charging $200 PCI rate, that Half Page or 6 columns x 10.5" size ad will cost you $12,600. Formula: 6 columns x 10.5 = 63" total. 63" x $200 = $12,600. To figure the cost for Magazines are pretty straight forward: Unit size x # of insertions (# of times run) = total cost.**

b) Non-traditional vehicles are vehicles, which as the name implied are not traditional media. It could include indoor advertising such as mall kiosks, bathroom advertising and in-theater advertising such as: posters and thirty-second (:30) spots airing before the start of the movie. These are only a few. The main function is to capture the target audience (or customer) while they are engaged in some lifestyle habits. These vehicles perform very well. However, it is sometimes difficult to gauge results because in many cases a third party does not measure them, yet. However, you can usually see a "lift" (term used to observe an increase in sales). Depending upon the media used, you can gain cost-efficiencies to purchase space. However, production may get pricey. Cost for these vehicles can vary. However, many will use a CPM (Cost-Per-Thousand) model to derive the total cost. Example: Advertising in a theater will be based on CPM. **For instance, if you want to reach 75,000 impressions (or persons coming to the movies), it may cost $60 CPM. So, to figure your cost: CPM x total impressions = total cost or $60 CPM x 75,000 impressions = $4,500.** Still other Non-traditional vehicles will use a cost-per-unit basis just as outdoor billboards. Just keep in mind to ask your media sales rep: "How are they coming up with the final cost." This way, you can check their math (media) and question the final number with some intelligence as to how they are coming up with it. This puts you in the know!!

c) Emerging Media are vehicles that usually involve the Internet. These vehicles could be: e-newsletters, microsite (this a miniature version of your website housed on another website such as a local TV or radio station website), Ad Words campaign (search engine marketing), banner ads, CMR (customer retention marketing) and the list goes on. Emerging Media offers the best ROI (return on investment) and tracking capabilities that traditional and non-traditional cannot offer. From a cost standpoint, emerging media will range in price depending on what you are proposing to buy. In many cases, a CPM model (cost structure) is being utilized. You can buy a certain number of guaranteed impressions based on a CPM. In some instances, you can buy a sponsorship based on a dollar amount. It will depend if you are geo-targeting (buying only in your local area) on Google™ or your local newspaper's website which cost model they are using for the unit you are considering purchasing. Either way, you can follow the math as to how they came up with the total cost.

Now that the categories have been outlines, let's review the individual media:

a) Television: It is a broad reach vehicle. Typically it is costly to purchase. However, it offers the benefit of targeting a specific customer by the programming. Daytime soaps tend to skew females where as sports programming tends to skew males. Television can be purchased on a local level as well as nationally. (National purchases mean that the commercial will air across the US. In many cases, small businesses that offer specific product or services will in all likelihood involve purchasing on a local level or as we call it spot TV.) Television will have the most viewers because there is no charge to audiences to receive the over the air signal.

b) Cable Television: It can be purchased to target a specific target audience by network. Some networks skew male, such as: Spike, ESPN. Whereas, other networks will appeal to females, such as: WE,

Lifetime. Then you have networks that have a good blend of males and females watching the network: TNT, TBS, and AMC. There are even networks for children and teens; such as: Nickelodeon, ABC Family. Cable tends to be cost-efficient to purchase since you can target specific areas of a city by purchasing the system in your trading area only. You do not have to purchase the entire interconnect (city wide) if you do not want to. It's also can be purchased nationally too. Local over the air channels (NBC, ABC, CW, CBS, FOX) are also available on cable. The total number of viewers reached is based on subscribers that purchase cable services. NOTE: There are alternative delivery systems (ADS) available in lieu of Cable; which is called Satellite services through DishTV or DirecTV. This service is based on subscribers too. However, satellite doesn't allow local insertion of commercials. So, if you own "ABC Hardware store" in Goodtown, USA, you wouldn't be able to purchase an ad on satellite to air only in Goodtown, USA. However, you can on Cable.

c) Radio: This is a very effective vehicle and affordable. It offers promotional tie-ins or remotes to assist in driving traffic to your location. Listenership is very high during summer months when people are out and about. You can target male or female listeners by format. Females tend to prefer to listen to stations formats such as: Adult Contemporary, CHR (Contemporary Hits Rock), Urban Contemporary, Country and Hot AC. Whereas, Males tend to prefer: Urban Contemporary, Classic Rock, Alternative Rock and Country. Of course, the target audience or age group that you are targeting depends greatly on which radio stations format you ultimately end up selecting. Additionally targeting can be used to reach African Americans with Urban/R&B or Jazz formats and Hispanics with Spanish-language radio. NOTE: Urban, R&B and Hip Hop are no longer just formats that African-Americans listen to these days. These formats are now appealing to a diverse group coming from all walks of life and ranging through various ages. Remember, we spoke earlier about Urban Hustlers, as defined by Alloy Access™. This group tends to embrace Hip Hop and Urban formatted stations. Now, I am not saying it is the only thing they will listen to. However, it should be something you factor in if you are targeting a younger demographic.

d) Outdoor: This vehicle has expanded to mean a variety of media. Many, now, dub outdoor as out-of-home. Although, it is used interchangeably. But, for this minute, we will keep it simple as Outdoor to mean: Billboards (Bulletins and Posters) as seen on/off the interstate and on local streets. Outdoor has the capacity to be used as directional signage, call to action (means: getting the target to act on your message immediately) and generate awareness of your product/service or location. Great medium to use but production can be somewhat expensive.

e) Newspaper: **ATTENTION SHOPPERS** - This is a medium that skews older!! Unless you are looking at using the newspaper's website too in order to capture a lot of young readers, you will in all cases end up with a group of reader between the ages of 25-54. However, don't get me wrong, it still has its place in the mix. It offers quick changes since many newspapers print daily or weekly. It could be good direct response vehicle (a means to get your customer to respond immediately to your ad) because you can advertise an upcoming sale. However, it can be expensive to purchase space. And, remember, you must plan to run multiple times in order to capture the attention of your potential customer. This is based on years of research that found that three (3) times is a minimum number of times. Unless you plan on running a large size ad for a special event that is being supported by other media, then, the one could serve the purpose.

f) Internet: This emerging media has taken off. It has re-vamped how it can be purchased which in many cases allows cost-efficient means to purchase it. You can quickly determine your ROI (return on investment). It offers a proliferation of choices: banner ads (which are good but fading in preferred choice and moving more into video and mobile applications) to e-newsletters, microsites, etc. (Remember, I said a microsite is a website in a website. You can have a small version of your website located in say your local newspaper's website, too.) Also, available are webinars (on-demand informational videos), AdWords or Search Engine Marketing, sweepstakes and more.

g) Direct Mail: This is another direct response medium. It allows you to track responses and the impact it has on sales. Very effective and but you must always have a strong call to action which normally involves price. Direct Mail can be very creative in what gets sent out. However, that usually involves more production cost to produce the piece. Postcards work well vs. sending a letter. Most consumers like quick reads because they are inundated with media all day long. **NOTE: Direct Mail's cost is usually derived on a CPM basis too. Whomever you purchase your list from they will charge you based on CPM.**

Within all these media vehicles, research on total audience, age group, household income (HHI), etc. can be provided by the sale representative that you are working with. The sale rep can offer you some assistance by providing options on how to effectively target your audience base using their vehicle.

With that covered, you are wondering: "What do you buy?" This is a bit complicated. It greatly depends upon on what you are trying to accomplish.

Illustration

This brings to mind another client I had who had a very small budget but wanted to create awareness for their new bank location. Of course, driving traffic into the bank to open commercial and individual accounts is the problem they wanted to solve. This bank just moved into a major metro area (affluent suburb) and was competing with twenty-three (23) other banks. As an $80 million dollar bank, they really had no chops compared to a $600 million dollar bank located right across the street. Additionally, we only had a launch budget of $60,000. With a small sum of money, obviously meaningful to our client, we had to ensure we were efficient with their funds. We could not compete head on with their competitors; as mentioned the largest one located right across the street. In developing the marketing strategy that the client later approved, we built a theme around high school bands which kept in step with their "hometown community" branding efforts already in place with the main branch located in a bedroom community, roughly twenty-five (25) miles outside of this metro area. I stepped in to see what could be purchased with the money that would be effective. First, I looked at "zoned" newspaper that would hit subscribers of the newspaper in their trading area. Then, I decided to seek out high school band sponsorships with radio stations. As a stroke of luck, it turned out the stations could implement band coverage into their high school football airings. (Sometimes, you just need to ask the question even if it sounds crazy and see what happens.) Also, I had set-up an online program that would be an exclusive sponsorship on a local website for high school sports. One of the features that our media partner would implement on behalf of our Client included a new section online to speak on how to help kids manage their money and save it. Additionally, to reach economic development leaders and new transplants to the area, I recommended a local magazine in the trading area targeting, real estate agents, chamber of commerce, etc. Area residents could get information about what was going on in their local area. Plus, it was a big benefit to new people moving into the area. Not bad for $60,000 budget that also was innovative to solve the problem. I wish, however, I could say they approved all of the above. However, the client was nervous about maintaining the online portion, which would involve them working with us every month about refreshing the content.   But, they did believe it was a good idea.

Before you start shaking your head that you cannot do this, yes, you can!! All of the above recommendation to this bank client was within their $60,000 budget. Grant it, there was a lot of negotiating that took place to get it within the budget. However, it is attainable. I'll speak about negotiations in a later chapter. You can have discussions with media sales reps to determine what may work best for you. Remember, our discussion in Chapter 2 and 3?? This is where you have completed your homework assignment of determining who is your customer and how they have heard of you.

As you review these examples, you can see how doable it is to determine which medium to use. Your budget you have set aside will determine, in many cases, what you can place your dollars on and how much you can purchase. As a course of action, in many instances, radio will prove the most effective and the least expensive manner to reach your audience. The various formats available skew certain audiences. Let's review a few of the popular formats:

a) CHR (Contemporary Hits Radio) skews younger females and the play list is current hits. Playlist would include hits from: Fergie, Robin Thicke, Mariah Carey, Usher, etc.

b) Rock formatted stations skews male. Generally, there will be two stations in the market where one skews older men with a play list that includes: 60's, 70's, 80's and now even 90's rock hits and the other station is "Alternative Rock" which skews younger men. Alternative Rock showcases the gritty hard rock groups. Playlist would include hits from: Kid Rock, Lenny Kravitz, Cold Play, Avril Lavigne, etc.

c) Urban, R&B or Hip Hop skews African-American of all ages. However, some urban formatted stations have created a spin-off station that caters to strictly the young teens to young adults because their play list is mostly Hip Hop and Rap. Stations airing Hip Hop and

47

Rap have now a broader appeal due to the fact it has become a lifestyle genre. It includes white teens and young white adults because they have embraced the trends derived from Hip Hop/Rap that includes clothing, style and vernacular used. Remember: We spoke about this earlier in this chapter. Playlist would include hits from: Usher, 50 cents, Missy Elliott, TI, Rhianna, Chris Brown, etc.

d) Country skews male and females. This is another format that will usually have two stations where the play list is varied. One station will usually appeal to men and the other females. Sometimes dubbed "New Country" where the play list is the top current country singers and "Classic" where the play list includes the oldies country hits. Playlist would include hits from: Brad Paisley, Carrie Underwood, Faith Hill, etc. to Classic hits such as: Johnny Cash, Willie Nelson, etc.

TIP:

Best benefit for using Radio is when you have a small budget: The station will produce your spot as part of the buy. See, you have no extra production charges.

Television and Cable will do that too. However, it usually will cost a whole lot more to buy a schedule. At minimum, you would need to purchase 5 to 10 spots per week on radio. Run the schedule flighted; such as: on two consecutive weeks and off air two consecutive weeks then back on-air for two more consecutive weeks. You can repeat this scheduling until you have exhausted your budget. The rationale behind this flighting or schedule: It allows your message to be heard over a longer period of time thereby giving the listener the appearance you are always on and extends your money. For any bonus spots negotiated, it is recommended that it airs during your off weeks. This too gives your customers the appearance that you are spending a lot of money and always on air.

See, minute by minute, page by page, this is sounding more manageable. As your business grows, you can look to add other media types, such as: Television or out-of-home, etc. Many times, you would most likely look at Cable first. Cable would prove to be a better buy with the bonus weight that you can normally negotiate. Of course, this assumes you are now spending about $3,000 to $5,000 a month, at minimum on Cable. REMEMBER: Look to use online where it makes sense for your business. Online is very effective and can be inexpensive, depending on what you purchase.

Let's review. We have discussed how to analyze the problem advertising is trying to solve. We have looked at basic research that involved specific ages and lifestyles. We had a discussion on reaching your customers. With the conclusion of this chapter, an in-depth conversation has been had on the types of media available, its uses and cost implications. At this point, I think you are ready for the next chapter.

Chapter 5

Negotiations

There is much ado about negotiations. The main point to remember is "build the relationship!!" Negotiations in my mind are an art form. Most people believe it takes a charismatic individual to be good at it. Well, if you feel you fall short on the charisma, no worries. As long as you "build the relationship" and "follow the process" you can be "very skilled", if not charismatic!!

TIP:

DO NOT TREAT REPS IN A LOWLY MANNER. They can make or break you when it comes to cost, developing a promotion and/or providing bonus weight. This is what we call in the trade: "added-value."

Illustration

Case in point, I once worked with a teammate who looked down on media sales reps. Of course, he never understood why he could not get anything extra or top-level service from them until this saga played out.

I was working on a baby Bell company. We both had to cancel schedules. He had to cancel the broadcast and I had to cancel newspapers. Those schedules that we needed to cancel were already passed deadline. (Meaning, it was too late to cancel.) Now, where I choose to contact the newspapers directly, my teammate chose to delegate it to the buying group to call. (NOTE: The buying group in large ad agencies handling all of the placement & negotiations of schedules.) Of course, the buyers would not have the same sense of urgency given they were not on the receiving end of the phone call I received where I spoke directly to the Chairman of this baby Bell company. The Chairman wanted the cancellation due to legal copy in the television spots and newspapers were incorrect. Needless to say, I managed to cancel all of the newspapers where my teammate could not get the schedules cancelled. Mainly because he let the buyers handle something that a senior person should have taken care of. Don't get me wrong. Many junior personnel are very capable. But when you are up against a past deadline and a request coming directly from the Chairman, you should not leave anything to chance. Given these facts, a senior level person would have been able to convey the importance of the cancellation and offer a tentative date to replace the schedule. Which are what all media sales reps want to hear: "When am I getting this commission back??" Has your curiosity peaked as to what happened with my teammate?? Well, it took the Executive Vice President of our company to make the calls and kill the activity. I was later told by this teammate, I made him look bad. In actuality, he made himself look bad because he made the call to delegate and he, himself, did not place a sense of urgency on the request. It is better to handle something yourself when receiving information first-hand that suggest urgency vs. a third-handed request, per se, by the time the buying group received the request. REMEMBER: The aged old nursery game you played as a child. You whispered a sentence into the ear of the friend next to you and by the time it came around the original sentence had become completely distorted?? Imagine the buying group thinking by the time the request was relayed to them??

TIP:

Remember: Build the relationship. It's key to getting special request of this nature completed. My teammate never gave the reps much credence. Therefore, in a pinch, they returned the favor!

Now that I have illustrated a practicum, let's get to the basic of what you need to know. As you recall, we have discussed the finer points of your audience you are trying to reach. And, we have discussed what media they are consuming. Now, you have to go in and purchase the "said" media. Some of you have not been a "client" of say Radio station ABC; they will in all likelihood want you to pay upfront. So, save yourself some embarrassment and ensure that you are ready to pay for the schedule at the time of placement.

TIP:

It's OK to get the information and cost before hand.
However, when speaking to the rep, be sure to advise them
approximately when you will place the schedule. Rates will
change from quarter to quarter.

Once you have demonstrated that you pay on time and your
check, assuming you pay by check, doesn't bounce, the
Radio station (or which ever media type you are working
with) will allow you to pay on credit. This means the
schedule must be paid for after it airs. Usually, this period to
"demonstrate" your credit worthiness is anywhere from three
to six months. (Policies vary from media type.) If you live in
a small town/city where everyone knows everyone; well, you
can probably get credit right off to bat.

TIP

Anytime your check bounces for a schedule or you are
late in paying for a schedule (NOTE: Assumes you are
buying on credit at this point), the commission the sales

rep received from selling time/space to you is deducted from the rep's pay. Please DO NOT LET THIS HAPPEN! This will sorely damage any relationship you have built with that rep. Understood??

When you speak with the rep, always ask, "What can they throw in as bonus (free) for the buy you are booking?" If the buy is substantial enough you can get something my folks down in Nu Awlins (that New Orleans for you non-natives) like to call *"lagniappe."* That's Cajun meaning a small gift given to a customer by a merchant at the time of a purchase.

Illustration

For instance, in Des Moines, I was able to secure remotes for a client based on a minimum $2,500 schedule. (In a larger market, you would need to spend more than that to get a remote as a *"lagniappe."* But, with a reasonable schedule you can get these extras that could range from bonus spots to remote to promotional tie-in. Another Des Moines example, I once negotiated a remote for a client who never advertised on radio before for $700. You are probably saying to yourself, **"NO WAY that happened!!"** Well it did. It happened because I had just booked a very large schedule on the station for another Client. I leveraged that buy in order to secure the other client's remote. Now, I will admit, this is not typical. But, it does provide a sense of what can possible be achieved.

TIP

Again, the "relationship" you build do come in handy!! It is the key to your success in negotiating the best possible deal. And, you don't have to take a hard lined approach to achieve the desired outcome.

If you know, you will start advertising by a certain date, a few months out you should start establishing that relationship with the rep. It gives you time to assess the rep's capabilities that you will potentially work with. Also, if there is another radio station of interest, see that rep, too. You will be able to see which rep will possibly give you the best deal and whom you prefer to work with. It also puts a name to a face. It easy to say "NO" to someone you never met.

However, it is harder to say "NO" to someone you have met!!

TIP

If you ever decide to play one rep against the other, please

be cautious. You do not want to ever give the exact rate or

cost to the competing rep. Many times when you negotiate

the rates below what is on, let's say, the radio station's rate

card, this information is usually deemed confidential.

Stations' do not like having their negotiated rates buzzing

around town for every competitive station to see. So, always

provide a range. If a rep ever feels like you have played

them, buyers' beware! They will see to it the next time you

get the worst rate, which will end up being the worst deal

you ever closed.

In order not to set you up for a fall, I most communicate that

sometimes early on in the relationship with these media

sales reps (or rep); you may not secure the best rates from

them. I say this because as a new advertiser you have not

demonstrated your "worth" to the rep. What is "worth"? Are you a one-time only advertiser? Or, are you an advertiser that the rep can continue to generate a commission from? The good news is: "The more you spend, the more likely you will develop clout with the rep. The more clout you establish, the closer you get to challenging "status quo" on the rates you have been receiving. This does not mean that you won't be able negotiate remotes and promotions with a certain spend level. It just means it may take a few buys before you can actualize better rates.

TIP

Rates on Radio, Television and Cable will vary during the time of the year. Generally speaking, first quarter or 1Q (January, February & March) and third quarter or 3Q (July, August & September) are the cheapest time of the year to purchase space. Whereas, second quarter or 2Q (April, May & June) and fourth quarter or 4Q (October, November, December) are the most expensive. Fluctuations in rate or higher cost, are also seen during political elections, Olympics, etc.

It is important to give you an idea of what the "used car salesmen" of media sales representatives that you may run into in the course of advertising your business. Many media reps are creature of habit. They get use to receiving without having to break a sweat and may not always earn your business the way you have had to earn your customer's business. Don't get me wrong. There are a lot of hardworking media sales reps out there. As with anything, you also have a percentage of reps that are not the best to work with. Of course, the same holds true for my side of the business at advertising agency. All industries have their fair share of the good, the bad, and the ugly! Let's look at who makes up: "The Good, The Bad & The Ugly" in reps. Over the years, I have developed my own pet names for them:

"The Smiler" – When I think of this type of rep, a classic song comes to mind sung by a famous R&B group. This rep

will smile in your face and promise you the world on delivery.
They will attempt to sell you what you do not need to
purchase. Once you have paid for the schedule, they
evaporate into thin air…never to be seen again! If you have
any problems in the buy, they will never return the call. I
actually ran into "the Smiler" once where they did return calls
and promise to take care of the problem. You guess it.
They never did anything. You do have a few rare "smilers"
who will dare to re-surface and take a second bite at the
apple. But, make no mistake. "The Smiler" will continue to
smile in your face all the while having no intention on
following through. If you experience this type of rep,
immediately call this rep's boss and request a change.

"The Smooth Operator" - This one, I especially enjoy.
And, yes, another great song comes to mind; a very popular
jazz tune from a silky female vocalist. Like a
Shakespearean poet, unsolicited comments praising you to
the highest level in order to close the deal. Everyone likes
compliments. And this rep will play on the compliments,

charm and whatever else is in the repertoire to help up-sell you. "The Smooth Operator" will goad you into buying things that you don't really need. In many cases, this rep will package the items so smartly and make it so efficient that you may find it hard to say **"no."** Unlike the "Smiler", the "Smooth Operator" rep will follow through and ensure that all goes well with your buy. In some respects, you almost have to admire this type of rep. Watching them operate can be entertaining, as well as, instructive. I actually worked with this type of media sales representative in the past. And in each case, they were all very successful at selling and maintaining their business (sales commissions). So, they definitely are doing something right. Hence, why I said "instructive"!! This "smooth operator" wants to keep you buying; like milking a cow. He/She understands the value of the overall relationship on a long-term basis. So, in this case, as long as you can milk this "smooth operator" into getting what you need out of the deal and you are satisfied, it's OK. What you don't want to see happen is you are taken for a ride and you do not get the returns on investment (ROI). At that point, it's time to request another rep. There is no sense to spend your advertising dollars unwisely. After all, you worked hard to earn them.

And, the top award goes to the "*She-Devil*." **Gentlemen business owners "BEWARE"!** This rep will never entertain a conversation with your wife or female staffer you may designate to handle the placement of advertising. She is bent on wooing you with her feminine wiles, which she translates into more dollars or commissions for herself. Rarely does this type of rep follow through on ensuring your buy is executed properly. If something does go wrong, she will always blame it on an underling or some other unforeseen entity. It is never her fault. And, in all cases, she will be so convincing that you believe her.   If that doesn't satisfy the unhappy customer, she will resort to batting and flashing of her eyes at you. And, yes, she is a master at getting this across even over the telephone. Please know, I will call a spade a spade. Additionally, I have worked with a few "She-Devils" in the past. Or should I say,

I had to pass the "She-Devil" on to a male staffer who was a

"Smooth Operator". This is the only personality type that

can counter the "She-Devil" and beat her at her own game.

In each case, my "Smooth Operator" was able to secure

what was needed for the client. Plus, this "She-Devil" only

wanted to work with my "Smooth Operator". Always know

when to concede to someone else who can get the job done.

Remember, earlier I said the "Smooth Operator" was

instructive.   Now, you can appreciate even more why I

made the statement.

Of course, some reps will be bad just because they are

clueless. The main point of speaking about the potential of

working with a "bad" sales representative is to advise you

don't have to buy everything they are selling. Again, do your

homework on what's available. Remember there are good

reps out there. These are just a few sample scenarios so

you can recognize them on sight and not be afraid to request

another rep if they turn into anything just described.

The other point to remember, always seek out information from more than one media sales rep in different vehicles: television, radio, outdoor, newspaper, etc. Sometimes, these entities do have "fire sales". This is why it is important to get to know and have a steady dialogue with many reps. When a "fire sales" happens, they will call you and see if you want in. Then, you can take advantage of a very low rate (cost) and get the exposure you are seeking.

Chapter 6

Execution

This is the sixth inning stretch. That's right, sixth inning because you are halfway through this book. I trust, you are glued to the pages and finding the information useful.

Illustration

If you are buying Women 25-49 and looking at Adult Contemporary, Country and Christian formatted stations, be sure to contact all stations in the market and have them make a presentation to you. They will ask what your goals are. Goals can be driving traffic, generating awareness, grand opening, special sales period, etc. With any schedule, you will need a minimum number of spots to shoot for per week. Ideally, in large markets, like Chicago, a minimum of 10-20 spots should be scheduled per week. In a smaller market you could go down to 5-12 spots/week. (Good catch!! You may recall in Chapter 4, we discussed using radio and purchasing a minimum of 5-10 spots. Now that this example is providing more specific details on the audience you must make an adjustment. Advertising schedules are all about adjustments the minute more details are made known.) Many reps will offer to put a schedule together that will maximize the rotation of spots between 5AM and 12 midnight. This is OK if they do this. In many cases, you will end up with more than the minimum number of spots. Again, this goes back to that relationship and the reps ability to adjust the rates to make it beneficial to you. If you don't have enough money to air the schedule (or flight) Monday thru Sunday, then you can have the rep compress the schedule to a Wednesday or Thursday thru Sunday flight. Again, the type of product makes a difference too. If you have a seasonal product, such as a beach blanket, you do not want to advertise at the beginning of winter. The last few months of winter will make more sense when spring break is nearing or the proverbial "spring fever"! If you are a club owner, you should concentrate your schedules to air during PM drive and weekends. It may not even be a bad idea to compress the schedule and have it aired during

Wednesday thru Sunday. Wednesday being hump day and many young adults already start thinking about what they will do Friday night and the rest of the weekend. The benefit of compressed schedules, you have more spots airing per day to have a higher frequency of message. These are all scenarios that we in the ad game factor in when looking at purchasing schedules of media.

When purchasing the media such as outdoor billboards, online, etc. Frequency can take on a different form.

Illustration

Billboards – One board sometimes can be very effective if the location is right. Remember, it's like looking for a house or an apartment: location, location, location is everything. But, make no mistake, just like real estate; you will pay for prime locations. Additionally, it is important to make sure that you contact a minimum of three months. Otherwise, you lose economies of scale on the production cost you paid. Or in other words, you end up spending money on something that won't be viewed by your customer very long.

Newspaper – DO NOT purchase display ad smaller than 3 columns x 10". Smaller display ads will get lost in newspapers; unless you are scheduling classified ads. Now, there are exceptions to every rule, if you decide to run a strip ad, 2 columns x 6". Then, placement becomes the key point of concern. Strip ads are great if you are a small bank owner and what to advertise in your town's newspaper. Placing this strip ad in the business section can generate visibility. Or if you are a builder and what to advertise your website or location of new subdivision to generate traffic, you can run a strip ad in the living section of the newspaper. This will raise awareness of the reader and engage them in a section that is important to them. The reader could be searching for home improvement tips in the living section of the newspaper. Who knows, maybe subconsciously they really want a new home!! With newspaper ad, you must place a minimum of three ads to be effective. (NOTE: The number of minimum ads to schedule is based on my experience and third-party research that has been conducted over the years about ad effectiveness.)

Internet – It may prove best to purchase this on a sponsorship basis. There are many packages that are offered by the newspaper, television or radio station's websites, in addition, to Google and Yahoo!. The key here is to check with them all and evaluate their unique visitors per month, time spent with website, page views information. Then, you can compare which may be best for your company. For the small business owner, a sponsorship offers you the best value in terms of the exposure provided at a set cost. There are other metrics (cost to buy) available; such as CPL (cost-per-lead). However, the other metrics usually involves cost fluctuations by month.

Illustration

In Des Moines, I proposed a sponsorship under the entertainment page from a local television station that had the highest reach of Adults 25-54. Many females view shopping as a part of their entertainment, it's a lifestyle habit. This online sponsorship allowed the customer to download information onto MP3 player as well as viewing entertainment news on mobile phone. So, my client, at the time, would have been able to have their ad viewed on a desktop, mp3 player and mobile phone. This is what we call in the business a multi-platform approach that was fully integrated with traditional advertising, television in this instance. The price for this was based on a sponsorship that involved at minimum six-month schedule. The sponsorship online was negotiated as part of the schedule purchased on the television station. So, it was a bundled deal. Had we decided to purchase the Internet package separate, it would have cost the client more money. The overall dollar commitment of $50,000, annual basis, made the buy very cost-efficient. Again, this is just ideas on how to maximize your spending.

Non-traditional vehicles - These are a little tougher to place in one category of how to buy. In many cases, if you can purchase advertising by location or a few markets. The rep will usually walk you through the various options. The best thing about non-traditional vehicles, you can engage the target in a lifestyle habit. In many instances it is where they play. These programs are specifically geared to the budget you have and what goals you have. It can at times be expensive. Not so much for the space but the production cost involved is what usually stops you in your tracks at times.

TIP

Always consider the options and compare the audience delivered with the cost you are paying. Below is a formula we use in the media world to determine how much it cost to reach 1,000 of the target we are reaching; term is CPM (Cost-Per-Thousand). To calculate it: Take the asking or negotiated cost divided by the number of people reached then multiply by 1000 equals CPM or stated another way:

Cost divided by total number of people X 1000 = CPM

Reps can provide "how many people" will be reached portion of the formula. And, you will know the cost that you are planning to pay. The CPM can let you know which media type is more efficient for you. However, sometimes the media may be more expensive but worth it because the audience is highly targeted to the consumers you want to reach. As an example: You are looking at print, it will cost $5000 to purchase the ad (three times) and you will reach approximately 120,000 of your target with the schedule. To use the CPM formula:

$5000 divided by 120,000 X 1000 = $42 CPM. You can then do the same with the other media to compare the efficiency of each media type. If you end up with something that cost say $898 CPM, then you may want to table using that media vehicle at that time; unless of course, you have some urgent need to use that vehicle. REMEMBER: Compare apples to apples; radio station to another radio station, newspaper to another newspaper, etc. The reason is the universe (total audience) numbers will be different with each media type. So, it's unfair to look at a Newspaper CPM against Television CPM. Of course, the television CPM will be cheaper than the newspaper just because television will have more people reached. Does this make sense?? Well, even if you don't want to muck with CPM by doing the math yourself, you can ask your media reps to do the math for you so you can compare.

We have covered the finer points of how to execute some of the typical media vehicles you will use. We have discussed comparing CPMs and what minimum frequency you should attempt to achieve. So, next up is to speak about the second phrase of execution ---- Stewardship of the buy!

Chapter 7

Stewardship – Tweaks – Results

Now, we're cooking!! You have by now analyzed your target, you've negotiated a schedule and purchased it; all based on the methodology you formed from the earlier chapters. In order to steward the campaign, you need to provide a certain degree of oversight on the buy even after it is placed. This is where you monitor what's going on so you can determine if you are achieving the desired results. Typically, agencies do quarterly reviews. But, for a small business owner, you really need to watch the campaign either bi-weekly or monthly. If your schedule will last only a month, then after 2 weeks, take a peek and evaluate where your results are. If your schedule will last a couple of months, then you can actually review the results monthly. Sales are a good starting point of evaluating success.

Illustration

I once purchased a radio schedule for 2 weeks with a remote negotiated. It was for a local builder. The schedule ran with bonus spots airing within the flight (schedule). This was a $2,700 buy on one station in Des Moines, IA. It also had a promotional component negotiated in as part of the buy. The promotion involved giving away a HDTV ready flat screen TV at the remote as the big prize. Smaller prizes ($25 gas card, popcorn bowls, etc.) were given away during the 2 weeks the schedule aired. Now you are probably wondering how do you monitor the results. The success was judged on how many people stopped in during the remote and the week after the remote. Hence, how many names they collected to follow-up after the tours were given in the model and how many people signed up online to win initial prizes online. The remote was a huge success. This builder collected 15 names to follow-up with more information on the condos they were selling. That's more than the average 3 to 5 names they would collect on a given weekend. Additionally, many people showed up one to two weeks later after the remote and schedule ended. They mentioned that they heard it on "XYZ" radio station. So, this is one manner to gauge success. Remember to always air a minimum number of spots as discussed in Chapter 6. There must be enough frequency to ensure the results. As you can see, I also negotiated in online as parts of the $2,700 buy. Of course, my agency, at the time, was spending significant dollars with the station. So, it was not a leap of faith to secure that for this builder. You, too, can do the same once you start having higher spent levels.

There are media types that allow instant results such as the Internet. The Internet offers feedback weekly, monthly, quarterly and annually. So, any buy you purchase online, you can ask for the reporting to be sent weekly (if you are only scheduled for a month) and you can make necessary adjustments. The Internet allows a two-way conversation to take place with you and your customer like you are sitting in your family room chatting with a friend. Make sure that you keep in mind whose your target audience and what type of media they prefer to consume.

This review process allows you to tweak your next schedule and/or existing scheduling if the schedule is still running. Even a slight revision can enhance overall performance. The most important thing to remember is you **"MUST"** let it run its course at minimum 2 weeks before you effect a change. This is the **BARE BONE MINIMUM** amount of time. However, if the schedule will last a few months, then a month is ideal before you say a thing didn't work and/or make a change. There are a lot of factors as to why something doesn't work.

Illustration

A story comes to mind on another account that I worked on. It was a major public university in the mid-west. We sold in the idea of a text messaging campaign targeted to high school students who were ready to apply for college admissions. Yeah, it seems perfectly logical that text messaging and Teens makes sense. However, we stressed to our client that they needed to give something away to make it effective. We offered up several ideas that would have been better than what we ended up with offering the school's fight song and screensavers being downloaded for free. However, our client was convinced that due to regulations they couldn't give anything of value. As you can guess, the text messaging campaign never performed up to its full potential. And, it was eliminated from the following year's plan. Yes, "A" for effort can be given to the client for trying the concept. It was a great idea. However, it was badly executed. The client never gave much thought or effort on what could be possibly given away within the rules and regulations that they were bound too.

See how something so simple can make a huge impact on results. In many cases, the right media, the right target but executed poorly can yield the same pitiful results. Here's another example on the opposite end of this spectrum. I worked on a beer account in Chicago. This was when Genuine Draft beers were being launched from every brewery in the country. The client wanted teasers ads for the campaign. A teaser ad is a :15 spot that was aired on television and doesn't quite show the product but is meant to wet the appetite, create excitement and encourage the audience to keep watching just to see what the commercial is about. As human beings, we are very nosey!! So of course, these fifteen (:15) spots work. As the agency, we foresaw the impact of this launch. We asked and encouraged the client to over order on the glass needed to bottle the beer. They insisted they had enough! NOT!! When the product launched, it **FLEW OFF THE SHELVES** at the retail level. It was like someone stole the product right off the shelf. Retailers couldn't keep it shelved and the beer distributors were making multiple trips during the week to restock their retailers. As you can imagine from my "NOT", the client did not order in enough glass. The momentum of this successful launch was STALLED due to not enough glass on hand to bottle the product. The launch lost momentum because the customer got tired of asking for a product that just wasn't available.

Again, you see how something so simple can impact the results. You must factor in everything from other events going on in town that will compete with you if you schedule a remote, do you have enough product available and do you have enough staff to handle a run on your establishment??

TIP

Don't fall in that trap! When you execute makes sure you plan for the results…..a successful one!!

Illustration

Here's an illustration of when other factors contribute to an less than successful outcome: The homebuilder I mentioned earlier had another radio remote that proved unsuccessful. They only had seven people show up to look at their luxury condos. The reasons attributed to the poor showing were:

a) Remote was on opening day of a big inter-State rival football game

b) Time of remote was smack in the middle of the game

c) Location possibly an issue since it was so far out of the way

d) Downturn in housing and mortgage market

TIP

So, it's not always enough to have right product, right target and the right media. You must consider outside factors that may possibly affect your outcome.

Stewardship is important!! You cannot just place your buy and forget about it. You do need to watch, make changes, if necessary, and review results. These results will determine if you continue to use the same media vehicles in the same manner or you totally scrap the vehicle all together. This is crucial to the success of your business and deciding future media purchases for your business.

We're at another junction at this point. We have covered a lot of material. However the next couple of chapters will provide actual scenarios that really happened that I worked on in the past. The principals you have learned so far will be further illustrated to provide a practical experience. As my mother always said, "Practice makes perfect." So, let's go on to Chapter 8.

Chapter 8

Case Study – New Camera Launch

The basics have been covered! Now, it is equally important to outline how each of the steps in the process work together. I find it helpful to give an example from start to finish. The case study we will review is an account I worked on in Chicago. Do I dare say how many years……well; let's just say it was early '90s. The client manufactured instant cameras and wanted to compete with all of the portable cameras currently on the market. The agency I worked with was in charge of the launch towards African-Americans. For the sake of this exercise, let's call the camera "Pronto"! Since the launch involved the general market (an agency term to mean targeting everyone without regard to targeting special groups such as: African-Americans or Hispanics, etc.), we had to coordinate our efforts with that agency who handled the general market advertising to ensure synergy would be realized between to two campaigns.

What's the problem? Client wanted to compete within the portable cameras category. Plus, generate excitement and trial for their new product among current and new users.

Who's the target? There were two targets: General Market Adults 18-49 and African-American Adults 18-49. For this exercise, we will focus on the African-American Adults 18-49; which was the target I was responsible for developing media schedules for.

How to reach your customer? Research completed was clear that African-Americans, at that time, were heavy users of television, prime and daytime especially. The television programming that appealed to African-Americans viewed tend to be more relevant to their lifestyles. NOTE: Listenership is heaviest on urban and Jazz formats. Outdoor was particularly strong in urban concentrated areas. As for print, magazines had a higher readership against the target than newspaper. (Remember this was early 1990s. Media choices available are vastly different now.) Camera research showed us that African-Americans were significantly more likely to use an instant camera. It also demonstrated an affinity to the client's film too.

Mining the maze of advertising

choices/Negotiations/Execute   The media selected included:

1. Network television means this is television that is purchased nationally to run in all markets across the country.

2. Syndicated television means this is programming that airs on varies networks at various times; such as: Showtime at the Apollo, Soul Train Music Awards, etc.

3. National magazines are magazines that are distributed across the country; such as Ebony, Essence, etc.

4. Spot television means this is purchasing television in a local market such as: Chicago, New York, Atlanta, etc.

The umbrella television coverage of network television incorporated a promotion through on network station. This network, at the time, was airing the Sinbad Show. NOTE: Sinbad is a comedian/actor. The show had high viewership from African-Americans. Since Sinbad was also in the spokesperson for Pronto in the African-American commercials, the network television deal proved beneficial with coordinating a trip giveaway within the show.   Additionally, Pronto was used in a couple of episodes. This is what we call "product placement". The trip for the lucky winner was all expenses paid for 2 winners to travel to Los Angeles and see the Sinbad Show taping.   The other network programming purchased was NAACP Image Awards show. Spot television was purchased in the top 20 metros. These top 20 metros were purchased based on total population of African-American Adults 18-49.   (NOTE: Population information can be obtained via Census data online, as well as, contacting your media rep at the local newspaper and/or television and radio stations.) Programming included: Oprah, A Different World, and The Cosby show to name a few. Syndicated television included the purchase of Soul Train Music Awards, Showtime at the Apollo to name a few. Additionally, magazines buy included: Ebony Essence, Emerge, Upscale, American Visions and Black Elegance. There were seasonality factors to consider too. Remember we had to align the African-American plan up with the general market plans to ensure that the African-American flighting was on when the general market was on. Additionally, key African-American holidays needed to be factored into the schedule such as; Black History Month.

Stewardship/Tweaks/Results   What were the results of all of this?? It was a huge success!! Yet, the African-American launch outperformed the general market results. The client later approved Sinbad commercials to air in the general market schedules to help boost overall performance and outcome of the launch. The stores located in predominately African-American neighborhoods that carried Pronto rapidly sold out on the product. Sinbad went on to do several more commercials for the client. He had such crossover appeal that it was hard to keep up with the retail demand of the product. As with some products, fads come and go. And, our client did not have long-term goals beyond the first three years of the products hitting the market. Use of traditional media did get the job done. However, if we look at today's market place, we would have had to factor in the Internet and other non-traditional media to make the launch a success, most likely.

Of course, this case study may seem like a whole lot of money being spent. And, it was a healthy budget. However, the point here is to see how:

a) All the principals work together that we covered in Chapters 1-7

b) A live problem was solved by using integrated principals to formulate the media needed to launch Pronto

Even with a smaller budget, the process is the same! You have to consider all the factors and don't take a short cut. It will prove disastrous in the end.

Chapter 9

Case Study – Major Public University

I have mentioned this university in the mid-west before in previous chapters. But, it provides such a good story, I feel compelled to give a complete review on it. Plus, this example shows how to sell an "intangible." The first case study was a "tangible good" that you can touch and feel. What happens if you have something that no one can touch and feel but only experience?

What's the problem? Client wanted to increase enrollment at the university among incoming freshmen. They realized that enrollment at colleges and university, nationally, was down. Also, heavy competition among other colleges and universities and their location all proved to be a challenge.

Who's the target? High school seniors were of primary concern because they were shopping for a college/university or some other career track. Juniors in high schools were secondary to seed the message for the following year when they would finalize their decision.

How to reach your customer? Research completed was clear that Seniors and Juniors in high school were heavy users of the internet, love to attend movies (more so than adults), moderate to heavy television users, hanged out at the mall with their friends as one of their favorite past times. Plus, they were avid gamers. Additionally research showed us that these incoming freshmen already knew they would get an education but wanted to know what adventure awaited them.

Mining the maze of advertising choices/Negotiations/Execute The media selected and purchased included:

- o Internet was cast in the leading role. All advertising would direct the target to go to the website for more information. The Internet provided our tracking to measure ROI.
- o Spot and Cable television was selected to provide broad reach. Cable to target teen oriented

networks; included: MTV, ABC Family and Comedy. Spot television programming included: Simpson's, Heroes, and American Idol etc.

o Movie Theater advertising was purchased to capture these teens while they wait for the movie to start. Plus in a primary market, Mall Kiosks was purchased to capture them milling around the mall with their friends.

o Outdoor billboards were purchased in one primary market, too. These boards captured the Teens in their way to school and when they were heading off to have fun.

o Signage was purchased in the University's primary market's event arena. There were local and state championship tournaments for wrestling and basketball that was held at the arena. Therefore, Teens would see the message in a captive environment.

- GameStop™ was used to capture the target within one of their favorite lifestyle habits; playing video games.

The Internet was the umbrella coverage of campaign. The remaining mix of non-traditional media: GameStop™, Movie Theaters, Mall Kiosks, Arena Signage; and, Outdoor Billboards all provided supplemental coverage by capturing these Seniors and Juniors in high school in their lifestyle. The creative message (the ad created) was instrumental in ensuring the impact of the message against the target.

Negotiations were important for this client. I ended up with anywhere from 35% to 65% savings off of media sales reps rate cards. This extended the life of the client's campaign.

Stewardship/Tweaks/Results   No tweaks (or changes) happened with the first year of this campaign. It ran pretty flawlessly. However, when I reviewed website traffic, year one, it was noticeable that after television and cable television flighting ended, the web traffic dropped off significantly. The good news is that in year two, the drop off was remarkably less significant. I attribute this to the campaign was now in year two and the message had been seeded with the target. Also, GameStop™ was still airing a month after the television/cable schedules ended. So, the drop off would be less severe than the prior year. The client got what they asked for. In year one, the university had the largest incoming freshman class enrolled in almost ten years. In year two of the campaign, the freshman class was bigger. So, the results of year one yielded, overall, a 6% increase in application submissions and a 15% increase in application submissions. Not bad for a public university!! Oh, year three is in progress now!! The tweak made in year two was adding in text messaging. Since I provided this in an earlier example, suffice to say it didn't work since it wasn't executed properly and it was removed in year three.

Now, wasn't that a successful story worth reading!! See how lifestyle habits, if known, can be used to infiltrate the mind of your target when they least expect to see a message?? This is one example of how to sell an intangible product: "education".

Chapter 10

Wrap-Up

Congratulations, you have made it to the final chapter!! The whole purpose of this guidebook is to help you do your own advertising by applying the science that we ad (advertising) pros use in the industry. You have been provided a wide array of examples showing success and failure. It is necessary to show examples of what went wrong so we can learn from it. Think of this book a secret family recipe. The first time you use it, you have to follow it line by line, possibly doing the same close following of the recipe the next few times. However, at some point, it becomes more innate and you begin to add your own ingredients into the recipe that enhances the flavor. This guidebook will prove the same with you in time. You will find yourself expanding the possibilities of what you do to target your customers. In the end, you will become the "ad guru" of your business!!

Remember the steps we discussed. Always evaluate what's the problem and what you are trying to achieve. Determine who are your customers and ensure the advertising reach that core group first; before you go off trying to reach those aspirational customers you would like to have. The core base of customers is where you can achieve a higher ROI. Ask your customers what they like about your company. Ask them to sign-up for a prize giveaway so you can collect emails. This is a perfect mechanism to find out more about your customers' likes to enhance your product/service offerings while finding out what advertising appeals to them with an email newsletter which happens to list the winner of the month, if you are able to offer up a monthly prize. Remember the survey of questions should be no more than 5 or 6. You don't want to scare them off and have them opt-out of your email newsletter. When looking at media options, don't be afraid to experiment. But, do it in moderation to test. So, don't take a fast and furious approach when you test. Many successes come out of "gut" feelings. Of course, "gut" feelings also tend to come with experience. Common sense does have its place. So tap into what your common sense is telling you. After all, you used common

sense when you started your business because of a perceived

"need."

TIP

You do not have to spend a lot to get results. Be smart

about your spending!! The funds you set aside should last

you the course of your season (if product/service is seasonal) or

the course of your campaign or the course of the year. The

point to remember is that you want to cover a specified period.

Remember to see the program through so you have some basis

to review performance and measure your ROI. Sales are

always a solid basis to measure ROI. If you can compare sales

volume prior to or if you have historical sales from the same

time the previous year, you can see if what the return was on

your advertising investment. The illustrations provided in this

guidebook have been yanked straight from accounts I have

worked on. They are live scenarios with live persons making

decisions about how to spend their budgets. You have seen

success stories and some not so successful results. The biggest advantage you have over these companies, you don't have a board of directors or stockholders to answer to. You are in a better position to react to your changing landscape. Believe me, once you start advertising make no mistake, someone other than your customers will take notice of it. Do you feel your competitors peering over your neck?? If you get copied, it's time to formulate your next plan of attack. Now, you are probably wondering "why" I would make such a statement. It's working so what if my competition copied me. If you haven't had an economic class in college, the term is called "law of diminishing returns." Sooner or later, you would have to change your tactic because it will eventually become ineffective. When your competition copies you, this law kicks in a lot sooner. OK, economics class is over!

TIP

"**Stay true to the mission you have set for your company.**" If the landscape changes or the customers you attract start changing, be sure to evaluate your company advertising &

marketing goals to evaluate if you are still true to your mission. Sometimes companies do have to change their mission in order to stay fresh with their audience. Look at Tide™. It's been around for years. But the brand has always managed to stay fresh and attract the next generation of users. Look at all the variations of the types of Tide™ available today; from fragrance enhancements to bleach to other additives all targeting a different customer. Plus, look how old this brand is and how successful it is!

It's OK to test ideas. Just test with using a small investment. Testing different ideas allows you to explore possible benefits. Don't be afraid to do this. In many cases, we ad pros test many propositions over the years. Some work well than the other and some can just be ahead of their time. Another case comes to mind. Nissan™ had introduced the dual-door minivan years before it became popular. It flopped when they launched it. The problem was Nissan™ was ahead of their time with the concept. Sometimes you will have to revisit a past idea when the timing becomes more appropriate.

Another point to remember is never be afraid to be the first. The University I spoke of was the first to use GameStop™ as part of their campaign. Later other universities started looking at the media vehicle as a viable option to consider in their advertising. Yes, they were bold to take a step in something no other university considered doing. Yet, they were being copied later because they set the trend that was contributing to their success!!

As with anything new, practice, practice, practice makes perfect. So, do not be discouraged on your first try. Keep at it. Review the principals again and again. It will become second nature to you; like riding a bicycle. No one rode his or her first bike as a pro. It took practice on how to learn to balance yourself and steer the bike forward. Same is true with anything in life. You will succeed and remember to develop your relationships with your reps because they can assist with some of the legwork.

Remember that old phrase, "Nothing ventured, nothing gained!!"

Glossary of Advertising Terms

Here are basic media terms and definitions to help you "mine

the maze of media choices!!"

Advertiser's Copy: courtesy checking copy sent free to advertiser by publisher and reported in audit to arrive at a total distribution.

Affidavit: a document used in commercial television stating that a commercial or program ran as ordered.

Affiliate: a broadcast station not owned by a network but airing its programs and commercials.

Audience: a group of households or individuals who are attending, listening or watching something. It is often used to indicate viewers of a television program or another advertising medium. Audience measurements are expressed as percentages, or as estimated numbers of households or individuals watching or listening to a program.

Audience Composition: estimates of numbers of people viewing a program or time period, by age, sex, etc.

Audience Duplication: the number or percent of households or individuals reached by one program (or station) that are also reached by another program (or station).

Audit: a formal unbiased check particularly of circulation of advertising media such as by the Audit Bureau of Circulations or Business Publications Audit.

Barter: the exchange of quantities of commercial time for merchandise or services. Television and Radio stations use this method a lot, especially with restaurant advertisers.

Cash Discount: reduction in cost of advertising space or time for cash payment, usually 2% of the net cost.

Circulation: number of copies issued of an advertising medium in print; by extension, the audience reached by other advertising media, outdoor posters, and radio and television programs.

Classified Advertising: help wanted, positions wanted and other categories of advertisements appearing under distinctive headings, usually with special rates for insertion and usually in uniform and specified type of a single size and usually no display (if set in display, called display classified); most classified is not mass product promotion but applies to service or the sale of a single item.

Clearance: an affiliated broadcast station or cable system's pledge to carry a specific broadcast or cable network program. Advertisers are attracted to network programs as an advertising vehicle partly by the number of stations or cable outlets providing clearance.

Click Rate: an Internet term indicating the number of times which an advertisement banner was clicked on at a Web site.

Click-Through: an Internet term used to measure the success a Web site has in persuading a user to go to another site.

Commission: remuneration to a salesman or agent, usually in the form of a percentage allowance out of the returns from a transaction; in advertising, the agency commission allowed by the owner of the advertising medium used.

Cookie: Identification messages given to a Web browser by a Web server. The browser on an individual's computer stores the message in a text file called cookie.txt. The message is then sent back to the server each time the browser requests a page

103

from the server. The main purpose of cookies is to identify users (consumers) and prepare customized Web pages (offering information, advertising, goods or services) for them. Cookies can include passwords and Web site preferences, as well as a history of the other sites visited, e-mail information, etc. Cookies themselves are not gathering data, but they are used as a tracking device to help the people who are gathering information. More complete information about cookies is available at cookiecentral.com.

Cost Per Point (CPP): an advertising cost calculated by dividing the cost of one or a series of commercial by the size of the audience, expressed in rating points. For example, if the cost of a commercial is $50,000 and the rating for a program is 12, then the CPP is $4,166.67 ($50,000 divided by 12).

Cost-per-Thousand (CPM): total cost divided by the number of thousands in the circulation or market. For example, if it cost $10,000 for a newspaper ad and the total circulation for the newspaper is 125,000, then the CPM is $80 ($10,000 divided by 125,000 x 1000).

Daypart: the time segments that divide a radio or TV day for ad scheduling purposes. These segments generally reflect a television station's programming patterns. The most common dayparts are: prime time, daytime, late night, early morning, total day, sign-on/sign-off, prime access and fringe. There is no universal agreement, however, about the exact times for all these dayparts,

Duplication: that part of the circulation or audience of two advertising media that is served or reached twice by the same publication or advertisement.

Earned Rate: cost of advertising based on advertiser's actual volume and frequency (where these affect the rate) during a contract rate specified in the original agreement.

Gross Impressions: the sum of audiences, expressed as people or households viewing, where there is exposure to the same commercial or program on multiple occasions.

Gross Rating Point (GRP): a unit of measurement of audience size. It is used to measure the exposure to one or more programs or commercials, without regard to multiple exposures of the same advertising to individuals. One GRP = 1% of TV households.

Hits: the number of times a program or item of data has been accessed. For example, each time a user downloads a home page on a website that is considered one hit to that website. Hits also refer to the number of page and/or graphic files requested by visitors.

Home Page: the page that appears each time users start their Web browser. Users can choose any page on the Web as their home page.

HTML: abbreviation for **Hyper Text Markup Language**, the computer language used to create website pages. It defines the page layout, fonts, graphics, and hyperlinks to other pages.

HTTP: abbreviation for **Hyper Text Transfer Protocol**, the underlying protocol used by the World Wide Web. HTTP defines how messages are formatted and transmitted, and what action Web servers and browsers should take in response to various commands.

Insertion Order (IO): formal instruction from advertiser or advertising agency for medium owner (publisher) to run a specified advertisement at a certain time; such an order is under a contract for that (and other) space.

Make Good: the commercial time given to advertisers either because an advertisement was preempted or did not receive the exposure that had been agreed to and paid for.

Mechanical Requirements: heading on rate cards under which appear the publication's specifications about plate sizes, number and width of columns, screen of halftones, etc.

Net Cost: the amount paid to the advertising medium by the advertising agency (or advertiser) after deducting the agency commission.

One Time Only (OTO): broadcast of a program or commercial only once, usually in syndication (As an example, Law & Order, it airs on NBC then again on USA and TNT. The airings of Law & Order on USA and TNT are in syndication.

Open Rate: the basic rate for advertising, same as one-time.

Pre-Print or Free Standing Insert (FSI): a printing of an advertisement before its actual magazine or newspaper publication to give it earlier publicity; especially to inform distributors of the coming campaign.

Promotion Copies: copies sent to prospective advertiser or advertising agency

Quantity or Frequency Discount: price allowance for volume purchase (especially of advertising) at one time or within a specified period of time.

R.O.P.: run-of-paper position; any location or position in a publication convenient to publisher; distinguished from specific preferred position.

R.O.S.: run-of-station position; any position on a television or radio station that is convenient to the station; distinguished from specific preferred position such as: front cover in print or prime daypart for television.

Rate Card: card or folder giving space or time rates of an advertising medium and data on mechanical requirements and closing dates issued by the owner of the medium.

Readership: Expressed as a ratio of those actually reading to the total circulation of a medium or to the estimated number who see the medium; where the ratio is 2 to 1 or more, that is multiple or pass-along readership.

Rebate: 1. refund of advertising payment when less space is used than originally charged for. 2. Refund, as of advertising payment, because of error or reduced circulation.

Short Rate: adjusted basis for advertising cost when advertiser uses in a contract period less space or time than he contracted for and if the rate is not flat but permits discounts (lower rates) for frequency or total volume.

Split Run: two or more advertisements of same product or service inserted, in equal numbers, in the same issue or run of a newspaper or magazine, usually in equal space and position; used to test copy by removing all variables except the copy to be tested; may be used to test factors other than copy.

Tear Sheets: pages upon which an advertisement appears, torn or cut out of publications, used to serve as proofs of insertion, for study of advertisements, etc.

Tip-In: an insert or single sheet fastened by a hinge instead of a wraparound in a bound book; a page fastened in a book, periodical, or brochure by a thin strip of paste on the inside edge of the separately produced page.

www.ingramcontent.com/pod-product-compliance
Lightning Source LLC
Chambersburg PA
CBHW070408200326
41518CB00011B/2115